The Covenants of God

Inquiring about the Promise of The Lord

Yongjea John Han

ISBN-13: 978-1-7750387-6-4

CONTENTS

Preface

God is the contracting subject and the contract is a promise. There is a subject of the appointment and an object. It is not unilateral. There is always a price for promises. In the Bible, God speaks through human agency. They are chosen through priests, prophets, and anointed servants and serve to convey God's promises to man.

In the book of Exodus, the birth of Moses and the covenant of God through him emerge. God prepares the Moses. At that time the Israelites were living in slavery in Egypt for 430years.

God remembered the promise of Abraham, Isaac, and Jacob, and looked upon them. It was the departure of God's covenant. He calls Moses and sends him back to Egypt, finally escaping the Israelites from the status of slaves. However, it did not end with it.

In order to live as God's chosen people, through training and purification were needed. For their status before the Exodus were slaves and could not be free from their status for 430years. They were born a slave, grew up and had to die as a slave. They could not escape from the bondage of being a slave, of course. In this state, it can not live as a covenant people.

The contract is a legitimate transaction. It is a promise between the two parties that the qualified ones are made to each other. In order for the Israelites to live as covenant people of God, they have to escape from the slave hood and now live a new identity. God's purpose is to bring them into the wilderness. God contracted them through

Moses in the wilderness. God said that if you obey my word, you will be blessed. If you become disobedient, you will have to pay the price for your descendants.

God gives the Ten Commandments through Moses. This was codified law. However, we need to know that the God of the covenant is the God of love through the eternal promise. He loved the nation of Israel. In addition, God loves all the people who are saved through Jesus Christ.

Jesus Christ is the fruit and end of God's promise. It tells in John 3:16. The reason He loves the world and sent Jesus Christ, the only begotten Son of God, is that the world will not be destroyed, but will be saved through Jesus Christ.

Therefore, it is proved by God that the God who contracts the promise is the one who loves human beings. Contracts are of immediate interest. God concerns our characters. He knows well who we are and what to do. The establishment of a contract is now evidence that you and I are closely related. Since God is in agreement with the man, we are now deeply connected with God.

That is to say, those who have received God's promise as a covenant people. The covenant of God is inherent, transcendent, and eternal.

Inherent Covenant

Inherent means that God is always in charge of human history. God is worthy to receive our praise and true worship. God made the Garden of Eden and created a man and a woman to live in there. They were made according to the image of God.

The creator God is worthy to receive glory through all things created. Moreover, He continually rejoices to be God among them by his covenant with the humans. Therefore the covenant shows God's active character.

Transcendent Covenant

Transcendence tells of God's omnipotence.

God transcends time and space and transcends all history. God knows the end of the ultimate history. It becomes the subject of the contract. And God knows in advance the end of the covenant.

God is ahead of human thoughts is above them and works sovereignly. Humans are only those who conform to the transcendence of God by actively responding to the sovereignty of that God.

Eternal Covenant

Eternity means the beginning and the end. Jesus called himself Alpha and Omega. It means to be first and last at the same time. The Lord is from eternity to eternity. The human lifespan is limited. But there is no limit to the Lord. He is the eternal God. The covenant that God has made is valid forever. It is not temporary. It means that the contract is permanent. However, the covenant between men is not eternal. There are the beginning and the end of the contract between persons.

But the covenant that God has established is in eternity by being eternal truth. The eternal covenant of God is a promise made through Jesus Christ. This covenant is a promise made with his blood on the cross. Jesus Christ is the covenant of salvation. This accomplished the new covenant of God. And it was recovering. The Bible tells all these stories. It can define that a covenant to become a new creature in Christ, and a covenant to live as a chosen people of the true God. Anyone can come to God through this covenant. If you are a people of God, you must know and obey all the covenants in the Bible. It is an object of the covenant and of course things to know and things to keep.

CHAPTER 1

The Covenant of knowledge of Good and Evil
Genesis 2:16-17, 3:15

The Covenant of knowledge of Good and Evil

Why is the covenant of God important? There are about 15 covenants in the Bible as a whole. Of course, God's promises are countless in the Bible. Here, the covenants are a contract that synthesizes words of all promises. The Bible is the book that records the promises of God.

A covenant is a kind of legislative action in which God reveals God's plan to people in the form of a promise. As said to be stipulated by the law of God, this contract can only be obeyed. In other words, it is clearly defined as a law. This is the covenant that God set by law. And every covenant from the Bible has an instantaneous nature.

Nowness means that it applies to us today as well. The fundamental elements of the covenant must be parties, promises, conditions, and guarantees.

For the first time, there was a covenant before the depravity, but it was destroyed by fallen persons. So the covenant that appeared is the covenant of grace. This covenant between God and man is an important covenant that will later be unified in Christ and connected to his judgment and his second coming. The fact that we are children of God can be seen as a kind of covenant with God. Therefore, we need to know what God has contracted with us.

A New Covenant: Blood of Christ, Comforter/Holy Spirit, Second Coming

A Covenant of the Act: the covenant of knowledge of good and evil
A Covenant of Grace: a descendant of a woman, a rainbow, torch, circumcision, ladder, mountain of Sinai, salt, priest, the desert in Moab, David, new covenant

What is the first act of covenant? (Gen 2:16-17)

What is the promise of the covenant?

God commands, the fruit of the garden shall be eaten, but the fruit of the knowledge of good and evil shall not be eaten. If you eat, you will surely die. God promised the fallen man. The descendants of the women will soon be victorious: the eternal victory of Jesus Christ.

The official of this covenant is Adam and Eve, the ancestors and representatives of mankind before the depravity. It was the first covenant of God to put eternal life and death before man's will upon obedience and disobedience to the Word, centering on the forbidden fruit to them. God promised eternal life under the condition of human subordination.

First, as the promise of the covenant, it was first commanded by God: God is the commander of man. The order is not a favor. This means that God is the Creator and man is the creature. Humans are the safest and most peaceful when they are in the Creator when they are under the control of the command of God. We are God-given beings. To reject this command is disobedience and arrogance.

Second, He did not make 'robots' when he created humans.

He gave us free will. "The fruit of the various trees of the garden except the fruit of knowledge of the good and evil is what you eat." Here, God can be seen as a protector who has made a boundary for man. As human beings, there are boundaries that should not be overcome. It is a boundary that can not be transcended as a human. You must be in the garden only. You should not go outside. This is the domain of God's rule. In the garden, He allowed human to eat at will. People have given time to choose and eat. It is given free will.

Thirdly in the garden, the two trees, the tree of life and the tree of the knowledge of good and evil, are given (v.9). Satan tempted human who created. God commanded them that It is to eat freely according to the will, but not to eat the tree of good and evil.

However, Satan tempted them that the tree of knowledge can lead them to be like God. Satan said them that you can eat without permission of God, if you eat the fruit of the forbidden tree (3:5) and become like God.

Evil is "deviation from degree". The angel chief Satan became the source of evil, but it was a creature of God and began to escape from God increasingly. Evil has become a proud and self-justified god. Satan can go anywhere (Job 2:2). He entered the Garden and tempted Adam and Eve in the form of a snake. They were the first to be tempted. The first tempter of human was Satan.

Fourth, it could not keep the sinful man in the garden. The reason is in 3:22. A man who is to be dead by the sin, who has been deported from the garden to eat eternal life tree and he had seemed to enjoy eternal life for himself.

However, the result of the depravity is death. A human can not avoid this. Revelation 22:19 says that the Tree of Life and the Book of Life: those who believe in Jesus and those who have written the book of life will be restored to the lost garden. Genesis 3:15 the first gospel was given to fallen persons.

To meditate on:

A man weak in temptation, Romans 5:12.

The cause of depravity is disobedience and arrogance.

The covenant of God who gave the tree of life.

The first act of covenant

Do not eat the fruit of the tree of knowledge.

It is important to build the will of God

"I will never eat it. I will surely keep the covenant which God has made." Daniel 1:8

CHAPTER 2

The Meaning of the Rainbow Covenant
Genesis 9:8-17

The Meaning of the Rainbow Covenant

What are the characteristics of the covenant in the Old Testament?

First, it is typological and model. They all symbolize Jesus Christ and the blessings of Him. Second, it is the fulfillment of the covenant. For example, the offspring of a woman will have a triumph. If we translate this covenant Jesus Christ will eventually have a triumph. If you obey, I will give you the land of Canaan. It means a covenant made by faith.

Third, the scope of the covenant is limited to individuals, families, and countries. It is a very personal blessing, a covenant for the future of the nation. Fourth, it is legally binding. If you disobey the laws prescribed by God, you will surely come to pay for them. If God's ordinance is broken, it must come to him.

Fifth, it is temporary and ready for the future. Sixth, the Holy Spirit helps. It is used by God as an instrument to come to an individual. Seventh, it is the promise of the covenant. By covenant, God promises to man.

What is the covenant of grace?

By covenant, God practices the plan of salvation. The grace covenant is a one-sided covenant of love that opens the way for salvation by making a covenant with those who have no ability to practice the content. God, the Father is the founder, the Son is the executor of God, and the Holy Spirit God apply the covenant.

It is God who accomplishes this in history, and God's work can be expressed in the Old and New Testaments. The Old Testament and the New Testament are the books of the covenant, the Old Testament is the covenant of God before Christ, and the New Testament is the new covenant through Christ. We need to think about the meaning of the rainbow covenant.

What is the spiritual meaning that has been given to us?

First, it is a covenant that has shown a clear proof. The covenant of the fruit of good and evil and the offspring of the woman is God's covenant. The covenant of the rainbow showed the great love of God. The human knew the good and evil, and the fallen human beings entered into the line of sinners in full earnest and went into the path of corruption, and a great flood came upon the judgment of them, and all the earthly men were destroyed except for Noah's family, eight families.

This is God's righteousness, and at the same time, we can see God's will not to judge us as water by showing rainbows. God shows such a sure proof. You can see that it is the divine will of God who does not betray you and loves you to the end. Second, the rainbow covenant means 'always showing new things.' God's covenant is a new beginning.

It means to cut off all the old scandalous and sinful lives and to start new. There was no rainbow before the flood.

The rainbow, which has never been seen before after a horrible judgment, means that our lives began with the blessing of a new life. Third, the rainbow covenant means the miracle of God in the ordinary. A rainbow is a natural phenomenon that appears in the process of raining and rolling clouds.

God shows natural phenomena so that God's blessings are not far away but are always near us. God calls all things natural to be a witness to the covenant (Deut. 4:26; 31:28; Psalm 19:1). He uses it as a tool to show spiritual truth (Matthew 6:26-30). Fourth, the rainbow covenant means "the character of a beautiful God." Each country has different types of rainbow colors. Some countries have five colors. Scientists who are good at analyzing say that rainbow colors are a combination of thousands of colors, like seven.

It is not the type of rainbow color that matters. The rainbow is beautiful. It is harmony. Among the natural phenomena of the world, the most beautiful thing the light shows is the rainbow. The harmony of rainbow-like light can not be found in nature. Why did God show Noah a rainbow?

It tells us the character of God, the love of God, which is in harmony. We want to live a life of light, a harmonious life that reflects the whole world beautifully like a rainbow with the love of our life.

The rainbow is a testimony of God's love and a shadow of the Christian covenant. Since then, people have been thinking about the judgment of the flood, being more humble and thinking of the grace of God when they see the rainbow.

When Christians are caught in fear and anxiety, they must be comforted when they see Christ, the ultimate covenant (Ezekiel 30:3, 18; Joel 2:2).

God says that I will see and remember.

Today, we can live without being destroyed because the covenant of crucifixion, which is the core of the covenant, is blocking the wrath of God. God, remembering the rainbow and the covenant with Noah, remembers the covenant of salvation with the saints when they saw Jesus Christ on the cross (Hebrews 6:16-18)

To meditate on:

Do you think there is no sure proof of God in your life?
Do you think my life is not beautiful?
Have you dreamed the grace of God in ordinary everyday life? Are you convinced that Jesus Christ is the most precious person in your life?

CHAPTER 3

The Torch Covenant
Genesis 15:12-21

What effect does human-centered thought have on faith life?

When he first came out of Ur of the Chaldeans according to the word of God, he held God's promise and went out (Hebrews 11:8-10). However, he could not own a pound of land to be ten years after he had caught the promise.
At the moment, he could not hold onto the Word anymore and he had human-centered thoughts.

At the moment of thought, he gets caught up in anxiety and fear that Kedorlaomer may attack. At present, his condition is neither son nor land. He was nervous and there was nothing in his hand. Human thinking; material, pleasure, knowledge of the world denying the existence of God, etc. causes such a man to enter into the fear of the future, the path of unbelief to depend on others(Acts 5:3,4).

When does Abraham's stagnant faith gradually recover? Restoration/prayer while meeting and talking to God

To Abraham, whose faith has stagnated, God comes in and says, "Do not be afraid, I am your shield, the greatest reward." And God will tell you not to be afraid because God will make you victorious. He will give descendants like the stars of sky. From that time on, Abraham's faith in despair began to recover. Abraham received the answer of God. Faith restored through conviction and answers. We need to meditate Hannah's prayer (1 Samuel 1:26-28).

Why did God restore Abraham's faith?

He wants to confirm the purpose of the call again. He said, "I am the LORD, who brought you out of Ur of the Chaldeans, to give you this land to work (v.7)."God did not call Abraham to wander in the wilderness. He called for the prosperity of the seed and the Promised Land. We are the same today. God has called us not because the Saints in this world have called us to die while wandering around alone. He showed the will of God and called for grace and blessing. God has called us not to suffer in this world. The Lord also spoke. "I have come that the sheep may have life and be abundant life (John 10:10)."

What is the meaning of the Torch Covenant?

Torch-burns, shines. It is a signal that there are a person and an important tool to illuminate the darkness. God is testifying that He is alive, like a torch that never goes out. Abraham sought for evidence of the Word (v.8).

It is the evidence of faith. If we have proof, our faith is firm. There is a lot of evidence that has believed in Jesus. We need proof. God showed the evidence in a torch covenant.

Therefore we need our preparation in advance; Abraham's obedience and preparation.

1) Prepare the sacrifice. In the Ancient Near East, when people concluded a treaty between nations, they killed the sacrifice and split it into two, and the parties passed

through it, which meant that the two sides would faithfully fulfill the covenant and the offender would shed blood and be killed.

2) Abraham's obedience-an obstructive appearing; every time there is an obstruction in the history of grace, which must be dismissed. Abraham fell asleep. God is revealed in Abraham to show God's guidance in the future (v.13-16). Genesis, Exodus, and Joshua are both included in the covenant.

3) A torch passes through the chopped sacrifices. We can not see with our eyes God because He is the spirit. He showed his presence in clouds, fire, and smoke.

The passing of the torch is the passing of God. Why did not Abraham and God pass by? The reason why God has passed by now means that this covenant will be entirely up to God's responsibility. God is faithful in keeping His covenant.

4) Today we are also parties to the covenant. This covenant is intentional. It is a covenant not only with Abraham but for all his descendants.

The Bible says: "The LORD our God made a covenant with us on Mount Horeb. This covenant was not only established by the LORD with our fathers, but also with us here today, and with us." (Deuteronomy 5:2-3)

To Meditate on:

When I was discouraged, did God have any solid evidence of me as a torch?

CHAPTER 4

The Circumcision Covenant
Genesis 17:1-21

What happened before He ordered circumcision?

It is renamed. The Hebrews receive a name when they are circumcised (Luke 1:59, 60; 2:21). A new name is given and circumcision is done.

This is what happened 24years after Abram left Haran. Much unbelief occurs before that. However, in the text, Abram, who has undergone a long patience-testing, has made God a new covenant and the possession of the perfect God.

The meaning of the new name is Abraham. It means "Father of the nations." It is a new start with the change of name in the old age and in the middle of a desperate situation of 99years old. He changed not only Abram but also Sarai, the name of the future child. The name change means to make it belong to God.

So far you have lived your way, but from now on you do not live like that. It means to live as a child of faith, as a child of God. Abraham, Sarah and Ishmael is one family, but Abraham, Sarah, and Isaac are spiritual blessed families of God. Here, the subject of the covenant is God (v.2) and says, 'My covenant'. God teaches His name to Elohim: the Universal God who creates and provided/El-Shaddai: God who transcends the laws of nature and fulfills promises. First, the meaning of covenant with Abraham is 'to call what is not as it is.'

He had no promised child yet but he will fill his spiritual descendants so that he will not be satisfied with one child as if he had children in his arms. Second, it means a clean ceremony to join the new covenant with Christ.

The name is given by God. Abraham and Jesus were also given by God. Abraham is the ancestor of the Old Testament faith, and Jesus is the first name of the New Testament covenant (Jeremiah 31:31-34, 1Corinthians 11:25). Third, it means that all believers are given salvation after a new name (Eph. 3:15; Revelation 2:17).

After we become saved children, all our being is changed.

It is righteous by faith, not by the appearance of evil sinners. It becomes the people of God's grace. Each of us has a new name. It is a new name, not as I was in the past, but as a renewed new creation.

How was circumcision done as God's possessed people?

Every born man must circumcise after eight days. This is a time when physiologically the children feel no pain and the blood coagulates quickly. The condition of the infant is unclean for seven days (Lev. 22:27).

It is judged that it is not reasonable to give before that. And the eight days as redemption, the first Sabbath symbolizes the new life that begins with the resurrection of Christ (Matthew 28:1; Luke 24:1).

Circumcision is done while cutting a man's foreskin. It is a symbolic expression that emphasizes dispelling the foul of sinful sin. The reason women are not circumcised is that women are included in men (2:21-24; Eph.5:22-33). The effect of circumcision has been on both men and women.

What is the spiritual meaning of circumcision and baptism?

First, there must be a human response to God's covenant. God is going to give grace and blessing so much, but man must also react to God. Circumcision was done in that sense. Second, we are God's full possession.

It is for the sake of the people's consciousness to be distinguished from gentiles. By this, we are a child of God and united family. Third, the covenant of God is a remembrance forever. Fourth, from now on, we will be a mark to keep moral purity. Fifth, in the New Testament period, it will be replaced baptism. At that time, the Jews were physically circumcised, but the meaning of the circumcision was faded and they did not realize the spiritual meaning, but gave meaning to the act itself and misunderstood as if they had received great privilege.

The meaning of circumcision has faded, and the New Testament points out that this circumcision has no effect.

So they started to emphasize the circumcision of the heart (De. 10:16; 30:6; Jer. 4:4, Ezekiel 44:7).

Paul correctly interpreted the true meaning and function of circumcision in Romans 2:25-29 and 4:9-13. First, true circumcision is the circumcision of the heart and of faith is important, and here both Israel and the Gentiles are concerned.

In the New Testament, the physical circumcision was pointless and this function was taken over by baptism. Second, baptism is a spiritual circumcision. It symbolizes that I am crucified and buried with Christ. It is evidence of faith and salvation.

It is the circumcision of Christ that is not done by the hands of men but with the circumcision done by Christ (Colossians 2:11). It is evidence that I believe in Jesus Christ as the Lord of salvation and that through baptism I belonged to God's children in the Church. It is said that the baptism of faith done in the heart is important.

To meditate on:

Circumcision and baptism are God's covenant. By circumcision, I become the possession of God. Today, spiritual baptism, the baptism of faith, belongs to God. The possession of God includes God's will that God will direct and guide men and women to the end. It is the spiritual meaning that God will be the master of the person and will keep it forever and protect it.

CHAPTER 5

The Ladder Covenant
Genesis 28:10-22

How old was Jacob when he took refuge in his brother's house and took refuge in Paddan Aram?

The distance to the outskirts was 800kilometers, and his age was 77years old. 20years from now is the beginning of the old age. Jacob died at the age of 147. The age of 77 is not that young. We must see that the middle age of the present is a little overdue. His brother had married three times before. His brother married a Gentile woman. Later, Jacob was blessed with the blessing because he had heard the words of his parents and greeted his wife (26:34).

However, his brother married the third time and acted neglecting God's monogamy (2:24).

He became very insufficient to become. But Jacob, as God's chosen people, wanted to marry the marriage of faith and to keep the pureness. He did not receive the daughter of the Canaanites (12:1) but to select the holy pilgrimage.

How was his life?

It was hard training and difficulty to wait for him who left home. Jacob lived mainly in the tabernacle, and his personality was gentle. A good thing about his personality was his patience. Jacob has patience and awaited the marriage with faithful even though he was old to marry, and spent 20years in the house of his uncle. He left home with only one wooden cane (32:10). In the past, mother Rebekah always protected his side, but not now. Now he is alone. He had to overcome all adversity with his own efforts. To such a lonely situation, God shows to him a ladder dream and makes a covenant.

What is the meaning of the ladder Jacob saw in his dreams?

When Jacob, tired of the escape route, was caught in anxiety and fear of the future, God wanted to comfort Jacob even through his dreams (Job 33:15,16). In that dream, there was a ladder with heaven and earth connected. Heaven means where the God of the covenant is. And the earth is a lonely, fearful reality, the plight of Jacob. And the ladder means the role of connecting God and Jacob. An angel is a messenger of God. The meaning of 'ascending and descending' means that the human prayer is raised to God and God helps and protects the human being from it. Angels represent the role of bringing God's grace to humans (Psalm 34:7; 91:11; Matthew 18:10).

This ladder covenant is the ratification and succession of the covenant with Jacob's grandfather Abraham. It means that Jacob took the covenant of Abraham.

The covenant of Abraham goes down through Isaac to Jacob. The ladder means the coming Christ, the key to the covenant. After the depravity of man, the communication between God and man has been cut off, but Jesus, who is a spiritual ladder, has reconnected man and God again. In some ways, man can not come to God (John 10:9; Acts 4:12). We can not go to God directly with our own good works or efforts.

There is no other way. Only a ladder is needed, the ladder is Jesus Christ. Where is Jesus? He is in the midst of us. God sent Jesus, who is a ladder to the Saints. He sent Jesus, who is a ladder to those in fear and despair, who rescues us.

What comfort does God give Jacob?

'I will not leave you.' This is a word to comfort Jacob. It means God's promise.

It is the word that guarantees God's protection and always to accompany. The promise not to leave you is to give to Joshua after Moses' death in the OT and a promise to his disciples who will bear the mission of preaching the gospel remaining on the earth before the Lord ascends to heaven in the NT. It represents the divine will of God to be with us until the end of all that he has given us.

What thanksgiving and prayer does Jacob give to God?

Jacob acknowledges God. He realized that God, who has been heard through his mother, is now my God, not God of my mother. The meaning of God is here means that his thinking about God's presence is completely different.

Jacob's new realization is that God's presence has not only come to the altar where he worshipfully worships, but that he is in the presence of God where he lies down in tiredness, fear, and loneliness. This was a surprise to Jacob. It is the fact that the altar that man-made is holy not the presence of God, but the very place where God is present is a place of holiness.

Where I am is God's place. If I am at home, there is God, and at work, all the places in the field are holy places where God is with us. Jacob is never going to forget this thrilling and gracious time he has experienced. He sets up a stone pillar, pours oil and calls it 'Bethel; the house of God.' And he vows to God. If I return to my father's house in peace, I will make a vow that God will be my God forever, that I will give to God one-tenth of all things while serving God, and that I will live with a clear faith as God's chosen people.

Jacob is convinced that he is now with God's protection. He's afraid and dark days before he fell asleep have all disappeared that his anxieties are gone, and now he is full of joy. Thanks and praise is full of beliefs.

He was born again. It was the moment when his being was newly created before God. He could express the joy of being born again. He made himself a place to bless his vigor by pondering Bethel Stone pillars. God also has the same covenant with us today.

That covenant is the covenant of the ladder. Where we are, it can be a place of God's blessing. When you hold on to Jesus who has become an eternal ladder, the place of despair turns into a place of hope. In the past, the place of failure is now a place of joy. This God is not far away, but the God who protects us who are near us.

To Meditate on:

Have you ever made a confession of faith that Jehovah is here indeed?

What was your situation then?
Those who believe that I am the house of God are blessed.

CHAPTER 6

The Sinai Covenant
Exodus 19:4,5; 20:1-17

How long did the Israelites stay at Mount Sinai?

Two months after leaving Egypt, they arrived at Mount Sinai (3:15). There, stay for 11 months and 5 days (Num. 10:11). Mt. Sinai is a place to become chosen people by receiving the law of God and making a covenant.

This is where we will start with a legal contract. By this covenant, they become chosen people and they enter under the rule of God. It will have all the conditions of sovereignty, territory, people, and law.

The Sinai covenant is a covenant made with blood and is a guaranteed covenant that will strengthen the future Messiah kingdom.

What does God say before giving the law?

First, He has put them down with the wings of an eagle (Deuteronomy 32:11). This means that he has led the people with the arms of love. To give the law is to love the people. They have tried to keep it under God's protection by keeping the law.

Those who are under God's law are blessed. The age of lawlessness is confusing. But the country where the law is kept is not confused, always stable and peaceful.

The reason God wants to give the law is the blessing that shows the well-being and peace of the people and the good shepherd God leads them to.

The dominion of the covenant is God, and man is the beneficiary of this covenant. Second, He will make them a 'kingdom of priests' (4:22). The kingdom of the priest is the leader of the redemptive ministry of God. It is the first nation chosen among the history of redemption and a mediator between God and the nations.

But now the elected people lose their privilege by disobedience (Rom. 11:20), and this privilege is given to spiritual Israel, or to all believers today (1 Peter 2:9). We have become spiritual priests.

To perform a spiritual priesthood duty, you must keep what God says. There are many laws about sanctification in Sinai. God asks the spiritual Israelites to observe the law of holiness. Without sanctification contracts, we can not associate with the holy God (2 Corinthians 6:14-18). It is not only external sanctification but internal sanctification.

There is a saying in verse 19:10 'Wash your clothes'. The meaning of cleaning clothes is a sacred ceremony for inner sanctification. But in the New Testament, Jesus says that we should wash our clothes. This garment is linked to the word that you should wash your heart's clothes by soaking in the blood of the Lamb (Revelation 7:14). It is not cleaning the outer clothes as in the Old Testament but the clothes of the heart to keep the defects in nature, but only as a blood of the lamb cleanly washed. The first start of the Sinai covenant is the holiness of the Saints. Most of the law is not near to the unclean (19:13,15).

What is the first word of the law given to man by God who has made a covenant?

It is the Ten Commandments.

It is also called the Word of God. The essence of the Ten Commandments is 'sanctification'.

In order to be sanctified and to live as a covenant people, we must keep this commandment. The Ten Commandments have begun to reappear in today. Because now is the time when this age demands holiness.

The closer to the end is the closest to being fallen. It is not sanctified, and the time age becomes obscene. The saints will live a life that can not be distinguished from the world.

So God calls us to build our faith again through the Ten Commandments. The First Commandment emphasizes the uniqueness of God.

He tells us to discard all polytheism, idolatry, pantheism (the idea that God is everywhere in the world) philosophy. There is no other god besides God. It is the beginning of faith to acknowledge one God. The second commandment is the ban on idolatry.

That is, do not serve any of the sky, the earth below, or the water below the ground. God expresses that he is jealous. The word jealousy means that a person loves and serves God alone. How much do I love God? Love gives birth to obedience, and hatred produces rebellion. If you hate God, he will reject you. The words to the third and fourth generations mean that grace is greater than the wrath of God.

The third commandment is to fear the Holy Name of God. God gives us many names. Inside that name is the character of God. One must praise God's name through pure prayer and praise. The fourth commandment is Sabbath observance.

Observance of the Sabbath means the best of the sanctified life of the saints. Keeping the Sabbath is like a profession of faith confessing that I am a sanctified person, a separate person, of God's people.

The fifth commandment honors your parents. Martin Luther considered his parents to be God's agents. Here, the meaning of the parents extends not only to the meaning of simple blood relations but also to the teachers and adults who help them for spiritual life (2 Kings 2:12).

Do not murder on the sixth commandment. It means to love a man as he knows God's dignity of life. Do not commit adultery in the seventh commandment.

Adultery is a blasphemy act and it is strictly forbidden. Do not steal anything in the eighth commandment. The prohibition of stealing is not limited to property but extends to all areas of life. It is the act of stealing to accumulate wealth in an improper way, to exploit the spiritual part of a person. Do not give false testimony to the ninth commandment because false evidence can lead to wrongful misunderstanding and death. The tenth commandment is about coveting. This means that God knows all the human minds.

Covetousness is not only transferred to action, but also it should not allow the mind to take others. The Ten Commandments are the laws that have made the Sinai covenant and given it immediately.

All ancient laws are based on the Ten Commandments. It is the most precious law, and it is a blessed law that the saints in this age must think and observe again.

To meditate on:

Let's take a moment to think about holiness in my faith.

CHAPTER 7

**The Salt Covenant
Numbers 18:19-20**

How can we go before God, through man (priest), or according to the time when anyone can come before Him?

Reformers who as Martin Luther, John Calvin, said the mediator for the confession and forgiveness of sin is Christ, anyone can come to Him, and church workers are the guides who proclaim and teach the Word and guide the Saints to Christ. However, Catholic (Roman Catholic) defines only a priest can stand before God as the mediator for forgiveness of sin between God and human. They stress that a confession of sin can be made only in front of the priest. When a priest forgives sins, he is forgiven. There is no remission of sins without a confession (sacrament to confess sin to the priest). We need to find the word in the Bible.

The Bible says: "Therefore, we have a great high priest, who is ascending, Jesus, the Son of God. Let us hold fast to our faith. The high priest who is in us is not the one who can not sympathize with our weaknesses. He is just as tempted in all things but without sin. Therefore, we shall receive mercy and boldly go forth before the throne of grace to obtain grace to help us along the time (Hebrews 4:14-16)."

When is salt used?

In the Palestinian region, salt is used not only to make food but also to establish agreements. The salt used here means faithfulness, the eternity of the contract. In Lev. 2:13, when they give a grain offering, they must put salt. This salt is called the covenant salt, and in Exodus 30:35 it is used as the ingredient of the incense used in the sanctuary. It means that the unchanging covenant of God, and the will of God to us to keep the sanctification.

Why did they think that salt could prevent corruption?

We can prevent the corruption of worship that we have to offer truthfully. In verse 1, sin stands against the sanctuary and against the priesthood. This is the sin of the saints to worship. All sins committed in the sanctuary. The king of Babylon, Belshazzar, brought unlawful goods from the temple of the God of Jerusalem, making a statue, so that they would receive the judgment of God (Daniel 5).

It means that we have been prepared unfaithfully and have not been able to offer it with all our heart. The priest's office must administer the sacrifices, burn incense in the tabernacle, lay bread, and turn on the lamps. What is happening in all the tents is holy and blessed. This is a sacred duty given to the priest. This office is not just given, but it is the office given as a gift in verse 7.

It's not just about coming to church and attending worship. By relying on Jesus' word, a new and road was opened to boldly approach God. The priest does not control everything, but God comes to meet all the people gathered through the word that is proclaimed. Worship is not what the priest offers, but what I am offering. It is time to come to God according to the High Priest, the Lord. But with what kind of mind does it go? You can find the meaning of the Old Testament.

We must distinguish holy gifts and present them before God with thanksgiving (v.8). Everyone who worshipers must present the fragrant incense of heart and the incense of life will please God. A man who is close to sin has the scent of sin.

He has incomplete fragrance. We must rely on Jesus, who is the bread of life and the light of the soul. Worship is a sacred ceremony to eat the bread of the Word and yearn for eternity, considering Jesus, the bread of life. Like worship in the Old Testament tabernacle, the saints must grow and grow in the Word of God by eating the way of life of Jesus Christ forever eternal life.

And as it continues to light the lamp, it must become a life filled with the Holy Spirit so that the light of our spiritual life will not go out. We say that we listen to the Word through the worship service one day a week and return to their dwelling by the filling of the Holy Spirit. Worship has become a time of grace and the filling of the Holy Spirit.

Of course, it is true. He is gracious through worship and boldly advocates to God, who comes directly to the temple of the heart as a spiritual priest. But worship has a deeper meaning. Before you come to worship, you must always be filled with the Holy Spirit. This worship will be a comforting during the service. A person who lives for a week and whose grace is in Jesus Christ know what a grace is and he can receive grace through worship. This person will spend another week. It is fortunate to see that there is an opportunity for the spirit to be restored.

God is the center of worship. If you are the center of worship, everything should be self-centered. It must be a word of comfort to you. Praise must be self-centered. This faith is still a fledgling stage. For those who had met Jesus for the first time (those who have different diseases, those who live with the problems of life), that was the place for them. Jesus also solved the problem by looking for them. But then what did Jesus say? 'Go now and do not sin again.'

This means that you should not go back in your sinful life. He is not tied only to his own problems, but to live for the glory of God. No faith should fall into you. It is important for us to attend worship, to be gracious and to restore the spirit, but before that, we need to be filled with the Holy Spirit so that we can come to worship. It is good for those who receive grace through the Word given to me and are filled with the Holy Spirit, but because they are filled with the Holy Spirit first, they must be graced with any word or worship.

Like the apostle Paul, like the saints of the early church. This is what the salt covenant means. All the offerings of the sacrifice should be salt. The salt-filled offering does not corrode even after long storage. It is like eating salted pickles for a long time.

We want to salt our faith. To put salt is to clean my heart. We must make sure that our mind toward God does not change easily. To hear the Word, you must salt it so that it can be kept in your heart forever so that it will be an eternal Word, a comforting word that will comfort you and raise you up whenever you are in trouble.

It is not a prayer to give temporarily, but a salt to be a constant prayer. You have to salt it so that it does not become a faith that warms up and quickly gets cold. The word proclaimed on our lips must be cleaned with the salt of the Holy Spirit so that the salt is add to build up, comfort, and prevent each other's corruption. Do not let the words hurt a person's heart by decaying "You are always like the taste of salt in grace 4:6".

Spiritual salt must be salted so that it does not change in many parts spiritually and physically, such as faith, hope, love, the Word (to be an eternal Word), prayer (true prayer), praise, service.

To meditate on:

God wants my unchanging faith. What can I do to keep my faith from changing? Let us consider God who made me a salt covenant.

CHAPTER 8

The Covenant of the Priesthood
Numbers 25:10-13

Apostle Peter said that you are the chosen people, the royal priests, the holy nation, the people that belong to him, that you may proclaim the beautiful virtue of him who called you out of darkness into his wonderful light.

You were not people of God before, but now you are the people. You have not received mercy before, but you have received mercy. (1 Peter 2:9,10)

How did Israel fall in Shittim? Who was behind that?

At Shittim, Israel commemorates the Baal sacrifice for the production of abundant grain and commits the fornication in the temple. It was sexually degraded indiscriminately. It induced idolatry. Behind them there was a false prophet, Balaam also called a fortuneteller. Balaam was a rebellious prophet (Num. 24:15-25).

He was the one who received money and made false prophecies. In verse 22-24 Balaam confirmed the glory and power of God in protecting the Israelites. So Balaam thought that he could not defeat Israel with external power (Moab), and he made himself self-destruct using internal disruption. The internal disruption was to upset the sexual corruption and worship, to blaspheme the temple and to destroy the faith of God.

The people of Israel fall into the schemes of Balaam and bow down to other gods. And they joined Baal of Peor. This means Baal in the province of Peor.

Here they commit fornication. There was a reason why they were easily tempted. It was because of physical and mental exhaustion in the wilderness life. Long-term living has tired their body and mind.

Just as Amalek attacked the weary, Balaam became tired and exhausted, dimming their judgment, and eventually, the people passed on to his temptations.

Satan knows that when our souls are fragile, we are attacked with a desire of comfort and pleasure. The fall of the people was a grave crime that broke the covenant with God. We need spiritual rest, fellowship with God first.

Who was among the fallen people? Through whom does God save the people?

Why did God make a covenant for the holy life of the people?

It is God's holy will that lives as God's chosen people. However, there is an incident that destroys the covenant of holiness. One of the sons of Israel came to his brother with a woman from Midianite in front of Moses and the whole congregation.

It was an act of spiritual discretion. Even though the wilderness life was hard and the continuation of suffering, it should not be left to obscene pleasures. Still, they commit crimes before the people.

Before them, there were leaders of the people. Moses and Aaron, in front of the people, were in before God.

It was a test against God and Moses. It also disturbed the order of the community. It was the logic of not being conscious of others to be together, but simply being able to comfort themselves. It was selfish behavior for oneself that had nothing to do with God's will. This is a scary pride before God. And it is a wrong act to legalize their crimes before God and the people. God corrected the mistakes of two men (Zimri and Midianite woman) in place.

Through Phinehas. Phinehas was Aaron's grandson and the son of Eleazar. Phinehas suddenly represents righteous anger at the unrighteous things that are before his eyes.

When we see two men who have committed fornication forbidden by God and have no repentance for this, righteous anger strikes them and kills them. But as soon as we kill the two of them, amazing things happen among the people.

In the meantime, the plague that plagued the people has ceased. There have been 24,000 deaths due to pandemics.

The pestilence was the punishment of God for the people to abandon God and commit the transgression of fornication. The unbelievable acts of the righteousness of one person have stopped the pandemic that has taken the lives of the people.

God did not say before that if the two men were killed, the plague of the people would cease. So far, things have been unexpected the events of Zimri and the Midianites in public, with their fornication, and suddenly Phinehas' righteous acts, and their plague, all of which were suddenly a great event.

What does this mean? It is an event that shows God working through a person who is awake. Not Moses was righteous, but through whom he had never known, the sins and curse of the people were ended.

What does the covenant of peace mean?

The covenant of peace is a covenant of the priesthood.
God allows Phinehas and his descendants 'high priesthood office' because of this righteous choice. This grace is given to the fact that Phinehas has removed sin. The peace between God and man is made by the cleansing of sin. All curses cease, and the passage of blessings is opened through the priesthood.

Through Jesus Christ, the High Priest, all the sins and curses in our midst are cut off, and the Saints will live with a new identity. We are the chosen people. It is a royal priesthood, God's own people. It has received a renewed position to promote the good virtues of God. In the past, we were not God's people. But now it is the people of God and those who have received mercy.

God wants us to be righteous like Phinehas. Everyone else is on the road to sin, but every one of us asks for a definite faithful decision to go with them. Just as the curse among the people has been cut off by one person's righteous act, and the promise of peace has been fulfilled, today we also have to restore our identity through the determination of a clear faith.

God introduces Phinehas like this, V.11 "He was as jealous as I am for my honor among them, so that in my zeal I did not put an end to them." This is not an emotional jealousy for God. This means God's own jealousy. It shows that Phinehas truly loves God. He who loves God does not compromise with all injustice. He acted righteously by loving God. As a result, the history of all diseases is gone. The people no longer have to die of the pestilence. True faith and love toward one God have opened a new way of life.

To meditate on:

Let's think about the sacrifice and love of Jesus Christ. Through His righteous deeds, all our sins have been removed. We are royal priests. We are those who have received new positions such as Phinehas. What kind of identity did you think my identity so far?

CHAPTER 9

The Covenant of Plain Moab with the New Generation
Deuteronomy 29:1-30:20

What is the covenant he set up in Mount Horeb in verse 1, and what is the covenant of the plain in Moab?

The covenant of Horeb is a covenant at the foot of Horeb. It is a covenant made in March (1446B.C.) after the Exodus. This covenant is a promise with the old generation of Israel. And the covenant was made in the plains of Moab east of the Jordan, about forty years after the Exodus (1407B.C.), and a covenant with a new generation of Israel.

The word "other than the covenant which you have established on Mount Horeb" means "in addition to the covenant made on Mount Horeb." This refers to renewing the covenant. It means not renewing the contents of the covenant but renewing the object of the covenant.

The Moab Plain covenant is a confirmation of the Horeb covenant and it is a repetition. And in the face of the land of Canaan, the new generation of Israel will remember the covenant of God, not forgetting the memory of the old generation.

What do we need to know to participate in the new covenant?

The word says that you must listen and obey the covenant (v.2-9). It is the footsteps of obedience to remember the grace of God that has been given to us in the past. When we receive grace, we become obedient when we realize. The first thing to know is to remember the grace of God in the wilderness of past generations. What should they remember?

They must remember that in the rough desert they passed through the desert journey with the care and diligence of God without any lacking (v.4,5). Next, they must eat manna, drink water from the rock, and remember that God has fed them. Who fed them?

It is God. God forbade them to farm for 40 years. They did not eat and live by handmade farming, but God gave them the experience to feed and clothe themselves. This is to enable men to know not that they live by bread alone but by all the words that come out of the mouth of God. Living with bread alone means solving what we eat and live while we reap ourselves.

It is not such a life, but that we should remember that we have lived by the grace of God filling us up according to circumstances (v.6). Next, it means to remember the event (Nu 21:21-35). We must not forget that God has defeated all enemies by walking in the desert. The people were victorious in any war because God was with them. It is what God has given them. We must remember the grace of God that gives us victory.

These three things must be remembered by those who will participate in the new covenant. Those who will participate in the new covenant (v.10-15) can participate in the covenant without discrimination, regardless of ethnic origin, regardless of race, age, gender.

This means that there is no distinction between being a Greek, a Jew, a circumcision, an uncircumcised, a slave, or a free man to be saved by faith (Romans 10:11-13). The word to be noticed is v. 15, 'To those who are not here with us.' It means us, not only Jews but spiritual Israelis in a broad sense.

It refers to all the saints and to the transcendence of the Moab Plain covenant beyond all nations.

What is the important content of the Moab Plain Covenant?

In conclusion, we say that God blesses those who obey and curses those who disobey. First, those who are disobedient will eat 16-18 a poisonous plant and mugwort. Wild plants with strong native and fertility are toxic. It gives a bitter taste. This is a curse on those who rebel against God with a rebellious heart. The seeds of disobedience spread among the people, and they immediately drive the community of Israel to ruin. Why? It is because the roots of sin remain in the community, such as poisonous and bitter grass.

What does the Bible say? "15 See that no one misses the grace of God and that no bitter root grows up to cause trouble and defile many." (Hebrews 12:15). Bitterroot is the result of disobedience. When these roots are established, the community is eventually broken. Satan sprinkles to divide. It is a symbol of the curse. The next disobedient vanishes the wet and the dry.

This expression means that the Jewish proverb says, 'There is nothing left to do.' The bitter root leads to an idolatrous worship of those who rebel against God and insist on living freely, and those who are strong in faith (wet), weak (dry), and do not be afraid of God's judgment, they will be cursed to become stiff. As it said in verses 22-28, God warns.

On the other hand, there is a wonderful blessing to those who obey. 30:1-2, when you remember, you are asked to come back. Returning means repentance. Repentance is, first, to realize and to repent of your own faults. Second, we will boldly return to God from the position of sin. Third, now, in God, we live by following the Word in Verse 4. God will lead us even if He is in heaven. Nehemiah also begged for the grace of God by relying on these verses (Ne. 1:8,9). God draws us back.

In verse 5, we return to the land where our ancestors occupied. You will taste the goodness of God and you will have the blessing of prosperity. In verse 6, you are circumcised in your heart, love God, and gain life. Eternal salvation is received. In verse 7 all our enemies will be gone. God will repay those who oppress me, those who persecute me. What should I do?

In the verses 8-10, if we obey the Word and keep the commandments and return with all our heart, character, and will, we will bless our blessings on all our possessions. It is not in the hands of men to live and die, but God placed me in front of me. So what do I and my offspring have to do well? You must choose life. We must choose love and obedience. It is a covenant of God's blessing to those who obey.

The Moab Plain Covenant is a promise given to our new generations. This covenant is still valid. Jesus Christ is at the center of the covenant. Through Jesus, God makes a covenant with us in the land of Moab. When we believe and obey the Lord God sent, we will be filled with the same blessing.

To meditate on:

He told me to keep the law. The law does not mean redemption. It does not take away freedom.

He gave us the law to give life. It contains God's justice, mercy. It is a lamp of life. He blesses those who observe it and do it.

The law of God is Jesus Christ. Now all blessings and graces are given through Jesus. We must be blessed Christians who keep the word of the Lord.

CHAPTER 10

The Covenant with David
2 Samuel 7:8-17

What is the background of the David Covenant?

He was in a heart to love God. David could not stand the fact that his palace was brilliant over the sanctuary of God. Before becoming a king, the humble shepherd became king of the unified kingdom by the grace of God.

If God had not been with him, it was a reversal of his undeserved life that he could not even dream of. After he became king, he thought that restoring worship was a priority (5:6-10). So they set Jerusalem as the capital and moved the ark to Jerusalem (Chapter 6).

The ark was the word of God. He promised eternal peace to David who cherished His Word.

And in verses 2 and 3, the ark was taken, and now there was a strong aspiration for the building of the temple (v. God acknowledged David's zeal.

He received David's heart toward God. The ark was in the veil of a temporary dwelling place, and his appearance in the ornate palace was still in the presence of God.

So he tried to force the building of the temple. But God's will and David's will were different. God received David's sincerity and entrusted the building of the temple to his Son. God is looking for those who truly seek Him. He who loves God truly does not break his will whatever he does. The problem is us.

How can I love God like David? We should not get accustomed to receiving from God unconditionally. It is important for us that we have a kind heart, and love for God with sincerity like David. Because David had this kind of heart, he signed the most important covenant with him.

Through this covenant, God led David to the stepping stone of the Redeemer.

What is the life God requires?

God imagined David's heart and positive attitude. He received his loyal enthusiasm and gave him abundant grace.

God is not the one who demands a man to be perfect. God is the one who receives what we are. According to their talents and their level and circumstances, God asks for a serious life that does their best before Him (Matthew 25:14-30).

God is the one who entrusts greater work to the faithful. You should just keep in mind. Through our thoughts, we build dozens of houses every day and we lose them. It is not just thinking to serve God. Though he (David) could not make sense of himself, he did not give up but loved God. He prepared everything for the temple building. God took this passionate attitude and made a covenant with him.

What is the content of the covenant?

First, in verse 9, God said, "I will make your name great in the earth." The name is the existence and personality itself to the Hebrews. The fact that God honors David's name does not simply mean that David's reputation is exalted. He will honor not only David's existence, personality, and status, but all his descendants. It is the children of God in a spiritual sense. It is a promise made through Jesus Christ, who was born to his descendants.

The name Jesus is the most honorable name in the world. No name has a more precious name than Jesus name. Wherever the name of Jesus enters it, there will be a restoration work where the home, the church, or the nation will be restored. Those who are sick are healed, and those who are tempted by the forces of Satan are freed in the name of Jesus. The name Jesus is the amazing blessing and grace of God who has been given to his family through a man named David.

Second, He prepares a place for David. In verse 10, God has appointed a place to dwell there. If a person's place of residence is unstable, he can not continue his comfortable life. Imagine wandering around without being able to live in one place. The place we live in gives us great comfort. The place to rest will make you feel comfortable.

God has prepared for us like strangers a place to live in the kingdom of God. "I have many places to dwell in my Father's house, or I will tell you, I go to prepare a place for you (John 14:2)." We went to hide in the wilderness. We do not have to wonder now. This is because God has prepared a new residence for us. Third, verse 11. "It will make you free from all enemies." This is not a temporary peace. It is not a ceasefire, but a lasting and complete peace. This is the peace made through Jesus Christ. It is the true peace of the soul, liberated from sin and death, and a place of rest (Luke 2:14; Romans 5:1; Colossians 1:20).

True peace can not assert my heart unless you keep Jesus in your heart. David was a mighty monarch. He was always with God. So he won wherever he went. The men who took David as their sovereign had nothing to worry about.

Because God was with David, he enjoyed true peace and triumph in it. "Your house and your kingdom will be preserved forever in front of God and the throne forever." (v.16) It is also important to whom I am with you. To enjoy the true peace of my soul, we must accompany Jesus Christ.

Through David's prayer, what we ought to be thankful for?

The right attitude of the saints is revealed. First, we must pray base on the promise (covenant). David always remembered the promise of God. And he held that word and prayed. Second, He longed to pray that he had already promised. David did not doubt and trusted God's promise ("Your words are true"). He loves God, believes and prays, and God is with David.

David is only a stepping stone of redemption. On the most important road to Jesus Christ is King David. We only need to know David to know Jesus Christ. Therefore, his prayer is the prayer that we must learn.

David's prayer was full of thanksgiving and praise. We can not find a prayer with complaints or grudges in his prayer. What were thanks and prayer for?

① We must pray for ourselves and for the family by relying on the name of Jesus Christ. "Now bless you, that you may bless the house of the servant forever before the Lord. The Lord GOD said, Let your servant's house be blessed forever (v.29)."

② You must be grateful for the redemption through Jesus Christ (v.23).

③ We must thank God and pray for victory through Jesus Christ (v.23).

④ We must thank God for the eternal God's people (v.24).

To meditate on:

David was a man ready to be blessed. If you want to know Jesus Christ, you need to know David first. David was prepared for the way of the Lord.

CHAPTER 11

The New Testament
Jeremiah 31:31-34

How does God fulfill the promise?

In Jeremiah 30, God makes promises to the people. The promise was "I must restore Jerusalem." He doesn't want God's people to suffer forever. God makes discipline when the Saints are wrong (the people of Judah walk away from God in a different way).

But that discipline does not mean the destruction of the eternal covenant. He will not forsake it forever.

Someday it contains God's strong will to fulfill and promise to overcome past mistakes and wrongs. There is a reason that God will restore the people.

1) Because of the intimate relationship. Judah was judged by a crime for a short time, but God decided to remove the pain. It is because of the covenant (Genesis 12:1-3). The covenant created a relationship between God and the people that can not be separated. No one can separate God from the Saints (the God of the covenant).

2) God's salvation is unconditional grace (Romans 3:23, 24). Because our deeds are righteous and not gracious, but because God has chosen and saved us sovereignty, the holy responsibility of God is here to save and restore the saints (faithful God).

3) This is because of God's absolute authority and love (Genesis 35:5; Exod. 9:14). Saints want to know God's love. You should not doubt his love. Do you love someone like me? Do not doubt that. It is God who honors my life precious over the world (God of love). The authority of love cannot deny us.

4) When we sin, we can easily fall into despair with punishment for sin. We feel despairing about ourselves while we look at the fragile figure that keeps falling often. This is the time when faith is tested. We must acknowledge our weakness so that we can seek God's help.

We must have faith. God is at the center of our faith. If we fall, we must rise again because of God. We rely on our own experience. We will try to get up with our own efforts rather than relying on God. It is because our centre of faith is not on the basis of word of God. We don't have any God's help.

However we will not overcome against all trials before us. Where is your centre of faith for God? God wants to restore Israel to make people realize that they are desperate and can not easily give up their lives. He raised them up every time they fell so that they could rely on God Almighty rather than their own efforts and strength. "My soul, why are you discouraged, and why are you troubled in me? Thou shall have hope in God, for I will still praise because of God's help." (Psalm 42:5)

What is the meaning of the new covenant God has made?

The new covenant in Jeremiah 31:31-34 is the New Testament in the Old Testament. The first place in the Old Testament where the New Testament is used is Jeremiah.

This new covenant is a promise between the house of Israel and Judah (v.31). It does not mean that the ten covenants of the Old Testament so far have been eradicated and made a new covenant. Ten covenants of the Old Testament are valid.

The old covenant was made in the day when God led the ancestors' hands of Israel and led them out of the land of Egypt. It is a Mosaic covenant signed at Mount Sinai, a covenant made in the wilderness. God wanted to cradle the old covenant and to keep the covenant well. Fallen humans wanted to remember God's covenant and be saved (Genesis covenant). He chose a family called Abraham and taught them how important the faith in God is (torchlight covenant). And he gave a faith to be an ancestor of the people of Israel, and to make them his possession: the covenant of circumcision, Covenant of ladder, established by consecration: Sinai covenant and desire to have unchanging faith toward God: covenant of salt.

He promised to renew his status (priesthood) and to bless him if obedient. And all these covenants were made through David to Jesus Christ.

When we look at all these covenants people should remember God's grace and live as a covenant people. If you do this, we will forever remember the grace of God. Having kept those who broke the covenant, it is no longer a covenant people but a dangerous situation that can not escape the curse and judgment.

So God signs a new covenant to renew the old covenant. First, the new covenant is a covenant to put the law of God in us. We must live with the law of God. It must be a habit to keep God's law. "The commandments of the Lord are with me always, and they make me wiser than the enemy." (Psalm 119:98)

Second, the new covenant is a promise engraved on our mind plates. This covenant is engraved in my heart and can not be destroyed. The old covenant is engraved on the stone tablets. It is important to keep it, but the people easily break the covenant when they have not heard and kept it. But the new covenant cannot do that. It is not a covenant that we can throw away when we want to abandon it.

It is an eternal covenant that can not be cleared because it is already a covenant established in me by the blood of Christ. God once promised those who received Jesus and became children of God. "After this, do not trouble me, for I have a trace of Jesus in my body." (Galatians 6:17)

Third, this new covenant is a covenant to forgive all sins. Through Jesus, we receive the forgiveness of sin (v. 34). It is God who does not remember again our sin. It is a new covenant to forgive sin. "We know that our old man was crucified with Jesus that the body of sin should die, that we may not slaughter sin again, for the dead are taken away from sin and justified." (Romans 6:6,7)

When will this new covenant be fulfilled?

If the old covenant required obedience to the law, this new covenant is a covenant that requires our faith in Jesus as the mediator of the new covenant. Now the law is Jesus Christ. Who should obey? We must obey Jesus.

We must obey Jesus' words, His life, and teachings. Those who have faith in Christ, not faith in the law, can fulfill God's promises.

Under the new covenant, I and you are the Israelites, spiritual Israel. The Israelites in the Middle East are still not accepting the gospel of Jesus. They are the people living in the old covenant of the Old Testament. We say that such a covenant has already been destroyed in verse 32. They still do not know the covenant even though a new covenant has already been established. We, the new covenant, are true Israelites. "Is God the God of the Jews, or the God of the Gentiles?" (Romans 3:29)

CHAPTER 12

The Blood Covenant
Matthew 26:26-29

We can not emphasize only the Old Testament or emphasize only the New Testament. The model house is a display, not a thing that people can actually live in.

There is an Old Testament for the New Testament. The New Testament is a commentary explaining the Old Testament.

The scope of the Old Testament is limited to individuals, families, and Israel. It is temporary, and the Holy Spirit is limited. It is a covenant of grace that keeps the grace of God.

New Testament on the substance of the Old Testament is grace and evangelical. In addition, it is a spiritual, eternal, and a final covenant. It is the conclusion of the covenant. The Holy Spirit works full to anyone, and the fulfillment of the Old Testament covenant of grace is the new covenant of the New Testament.

What covenant is the most important covenant in every covenant (Matthew 26:26-29; Mark 14:22-25; Luke 22: 14-20)?

It is a covenant of redemption of the cross of Jesus Christ.

It is a covenant to remember and redeem of Christ, who died on the cross for sinners, commemorating Christ through the Lord's Supper until the Second Coming. It is the most important covenant of life among all the covenants of the Bible. To understand the covenant of life, we must first understand the Old Testament.

① It is a Passover supper. If the Passover Supper is to commemorate Israel's salvation in Egypt, the Lord's Supper commemorates the release of Jesus from the power of Satan, who was the slave of sin.

② It is the blood of the lamb that is attached to the doorpost of the Passover. It caught the lamb on a Passover evening. And by putting the blood on the doorposts, it saved the Israelites from the death (Exodus 12:1-14). Blood is soon evidence and the covenant ("I will see the blood and I will pass"). God has seen the blood, and has not judged (death) in the house; Doorpost is door frame. It is a must to cross to enter the house. He did not tell the lamb's blood to the corner of the invisible house, but to put it on the doorframe for everyone to see.

This means that this house is a separate place of God's covenant. The blood of Jesus Christ, the Lamb who rescued man from eternal death, must remain a witness to our souls. We are a believer in the blood of Jesus. Our house is a home for Jesus. There must be clear evidence. Our home is a place redeemed by Jesus' cross grace. It is Jesus who protects us (1 John 1:7).

③ Jesus set up the new covenant as a new covenant with the blood of the Lamb, as opposed to the Passover celebration, as a new covenant made with my blood (1 Corinthians 11:25). These bread and wine that Jesus gave to His disciples meant His death, and His disciples enacted the Lord's Supper to commemorate His death.

Let's meditate on the blood of the covenant.

God has made many covenants and guided in grace to save man from sin. God's work was always consistent. It is a precise plan. After passing through Adam (Genesis 2:7; 3:15), Noah (Genesis 6:18), Abraham (Genesis 15:8), Moses (Exodus 24:8) and David (2 Samuel 7:12-16), the outline for at first it looked faint and vague.

It appears uncertain as the mist of the morning. Then, as the fog gradually fades, all things are clearly visible. In the process of fogging, God promised His covenant with grace. Why did the Old Testament covenant be called the covenant of grace? It was the hand of God who led and guarded Himself not to get lost in the fog.

Imagine that our future is uncertain and you do not know what to do or where to go. We can not change our minds as long as the fog of life is covered as we cannot drive a car in the mist. The Old Testament covenants of grace are like guides to guide our way of life for a new covenant. Live God-centered life. Be sanctified.

Be protected. Make sure your identity and obey to the covenant. Faith never changes. Do not forget to think about the grace God has given you. It was the covenants of the grace of our God who guided the right way through the covenants.

It is the blood covenant which unifies these covenants. The Blood in the Bible is life (Gen 9:4,5; Lev 17:11). Without bloodshed, there is no saving or forgiveness (Hebrews 9:22). The New Covenant of Atonement that will save lives to die for sin is established as the Blood of Jesus.

The result of crucifixion & The Blessings of Jesus' Passion

John 19:1-3; Thrashing, crown of thorns, righteous Romans 8:17, 18-Glory "to be glorified with him"
Matthew 27:31-44; trouble, crucifixion 11: 28; Sabbath
Matthew 26:38; sorrow-my heart is troubled. 16:20, 22; Joy: sorrow will be a joy.
Matthew 27:46; Forgiven - Eli Eliel Rama Sabbatani 16:31; Saved: You and your house will be saved
Gal 3:13; Curse - Cursed for us.
Gal 3:9; Blessed: Abraham with faith,
John 19:34; Bloodshed
Hebrews 9:22; Apostle: Without blood shedding, there will be no forgiveness.
John 19:30; death
John 3:16; eternal life: to have eternal life

Symbol of Crucifixion

1) Love of God (John3:16); God so loved the world that He gave His only begotten Son
2) Passion (John19:17-30); He directs his cross, and I am thirsty. It is done.
3) Humiliation (Hebrews12:2)
4) Sacrifice (Colossians1:20); by the blood of his crucifixion
5) Obedience and humility (Phil.2:8); He appeared in the shape of a man. He humiliated himself and was obedient to death.
6) Salvation (1Corinthians1:18); the way of the cross is foolish for those who perish,

73

7) Grace (Romans 3:24); those who are justified by God's grace through redemption in Christ Jesus
8) Forgiveness (Luke 23:34); Father, forgive them, for they do not know what they are doing.
9) Victory (Gal 6:14); I have nothing to boast about except the cross of our Lord Jesus Christ
10) Peace (Colossians 1:20); through the blood of his cross, he made peace, and all things,
11) The life of a Christian (Matthew 10:38);
12) At the end of the Old Testament sacrifice (Colossians 2:14); He cleansed the testimony written against the law against us,

if you have memorized the symbols and meanings of the twelve crosses, it will be a great help for your faithful life. You can overcome and win if you take the testimony of the Bible.

The charm of the world is to pursue demons with the power of demons (not to escape the power of the devil for life) Christians can defeat the devil with the power of Jesus' Grace of the cross.

CHAPTER 13

The Comforter Covenant
John 16:7-15

Covenant of the Comforter

All the churches and Christians represented by the disciples of Jesus Christ (spiritual true Israelites)

When does the covenant take effect?

After Jesus Christ is resurrected and ascended, in the Pentecost of Mark (Acts 1 and 2)

The covenant after the ascension they will continue to live with the Christians and will send the Holy Spirit of the Comforter, who will testify of Jesus and guide the saints into the truth (John 14:16, 26; 15:26, Acts 1:4, 5)

Jesus told us why he should send the Holy Spirit to us through the Comforter. What are the reasons? (16:1-6)

Through the covenant of the Comforter, Jesus promised to send the Holy Spirit. Jesus said this for a reason. First, it is to keep the remaining Saints from falling. In verse 16: 1, Jesus said of the covenant, "This is to prevent you from falling." After Jesus ascended, we can not see Jesus in the flesh. Jesus is already sitting on the throne of God after he has risen and ascended.

Before Jesus ascended, he showed himself to his disciples and to the crowds that followed him, but after he ascended, they could not see it. A person with a center of faith can keep his position without falling constantly, but if not, he or she will get stuck. They can pass on to Satan's trick to overthrow the weakest. So he promises to send the Holy Spirit of the Comforter to keep the remaining Saints from falling.

This means that if you do not lose your faith while living your faith, you must fill the Holy Spirit.

What does the filling of the Holy Spirit mean?

It is always thinking of the Lord in our lives and overpowering us. This is more meaningful than other mentions. Now we see the Lord with our soul, not with our eyes. It is in spiritual eyes to see the Lord in me. Those who have left their spiritual eyes will always live a life filled with the Holy Spirit.

We need to slowly check what the obstacles are in front of you and walk around. At the same time as paying attention to oneself, the fault also comes from the outside. Therefore, it is important to rely on the Holy Spirit of the Comforter in order to have a victory lastly.

Second, the reason for sending the Holy Spirit of the Comforter is to know "How can I do God's work well?" The Holy Spirit teaches and guides me to do the work of God. In verse 2-4, we must do what God is doing. Jews who do not believe in Jesus persecute Christians. But they mistakenly think this is God's work. They persecute Christians. So Jesus said that He will send the Holy Spirit of Comforter to teach those who do not know what the work of God is "this is the work of the true God." There must be a clear purpose for why we do this when we work.

If you think that it is wrong to do, you will continue to walk in the wrong way.

We have to give advice and lead them. It is our job to help them. God's work must be done in the right way. Only the Holy Spirit can teach what is God's work.

Third, He promises to send the Holy Spirit of the Comforter to remove the anxiety in our heart. If we do not know the heart of Jesus, we are grieved in our heart. Verses 5 and 6 tell us that Jesus must go to Heavenly Father, and no one asks why he is going and where he is going. They do not ask, they just worry. If our heart is full of anxiety, there is no day to comfort us.

Proverbs 12:25 "If anxiety is in the heart of a man, it will bring it to be defiled, but good words make it pleasing." The reason that a man can not hold his heart and wanders is shaken because his heart is troubled. Even with a little anxiety, you should not go over it. The more people think, the greater the tendency to grow. If you keep a small fire, you can raise the anxiety in your mind as if it were a big fire.

Do not let the anxious seed grow. Do not let it grow. Now the disciples are growing anxious. They are so obsessed with saying that Jesus is going to leave. Why are you leaving? When you ask the question "When will you come back?" And if you get the answer, you can live with hope after waiting for the next time you come again. The Holy Spirit of the Comforter is in our hearts. Jesus gives you peace. With Jesus in my heart, I can enjoy the peace of my soul. (John 14:26,27)

The Comforter - to teach and remind me, to give me peace, this peace is not the peace of the world, do not be afraid.

Fourth, the Comforter is for our spiritual benefit. It is beneficial for the disciples to leave Jesus in verse 7. What does this mean? Now it is an independent faith that stands up for itself by the Holy Spirit.

As Jesus is the one who guided His disciples before His ascension, the Holy Spirit, the Comforter, guides His disciples after Jesus has gone. And this man still leads our saints. He teaches us. He teaches about God's work, about sin, about righteousness, and protects the Saints.

Without the Holy Spirit's rebuke, we do not realize that we are a sinner. When I come to church and listen to the Word, I realize that I am a sinner. But it is not the one who makes me realize it, but the Holy Spirit who comes to me. And only the Holy Spirit makes us believe that Jesus died on the cross. He makes us believe in His resurrection. This is God's righteousness.

It is the work of the Holy Spirit that I believe in Jesus and become righteous by faith. And the Holy Spirit teaches that those who refuse to repent and do not believe in Jesus will eventually join Satan's judgment.

In the end, it is the work of the Holy Spirit to realize the sin, to be forgiven, and to avoid judgment, so that the Holy Spirit is the one who takes responsibility for the saints to the end and guides them from this land. The Holy Spirit works in the Old Testament, but it is partial. When God uses a person to use it, he gives a power for that they have worked, but now the story is completely different in the New Testament.

Because of the new way of salvation through Jesus, the Holy Spirit works for anyone who believes in Jesus. This is the Comforter. Like the great Old Testament and New Testament figures, we can do God's work if the Holy Spirit works. This is the new covenant of grace.

[The ministry of the Holy Spirit to the Saints]

1.Rebirth (John 3:3,5) 2. Evidence of Christ (John 15:26) 3. Leading to the truth (John 16:13) 4. Baptism of the Holy Spirit (Acts 2:17-41) 5. Knowing God's Love (Romans 5:5) 6. Freedom from Sin and Death (Romans 8:2) 7. Being in us (1 Corinthians 3:16) 8. I am a child of God (Romans 8:16). 9. Holiness (Romans 15:16) 10. To know God's grace (1 Corinthians 2:12) 11. Giving gifts (1 Corinthians 12:3-11) 12. Consolidating the saints (1 Corinthians 12:13; Philippians 1:22) 13. Freedom (2 Corinthians 3:17) 14. Fruit of the Holy Spirit (Gal. 5:22,23) 15, The Fellowship of the saints (Philippians 2:1)

CHAPTER 14

The Second Coming Covenant
Luke 21:20-28

We can find several verses about the Second Coming Covenants from the Other Gospel: Matthew 24:15-21/ Mark 13:14-19, 24-27/John 14

The Second Coming covenant that the Lord will come again after the resurrection is also revealed in all the Gospels and the letters of the apostles, and in particular, the Book of Revelation details of the Second Coming covenant.

This is the future covenant of the Lord's Second Coming, which is not yet fulfilled, and it is an important and final covenant in the new covenant.

So far, all the covenants of the Old and New Testament have been fulfilled. This covenant of the Second Coming shall be kept in mind until the Saints shall remember them and come to the Lord. The Second Coming covenant specifically tells about the signs that will appear at the end, why the Lord must come back and the attitude of the saints to the end. The end will make our faith stronger, win over the present suffering, victory, and hope for the future.

Why should Jesus come again?

The Lord accomplished his will in the event of the crucifixion. And through resurrection he overcame death. He ascended to heaven in front of his disciples. Now, through these disciples who have witnessed all these events, the cross, the resurrection, and the ascension, the Lord accomplish ministry. It is not all over because the

Lord ascended. God's work through His disciples has been renewed since then.

It is the time of the remaining saints who will ascend and come to the earth the next time (only the Father knows the time and place), and it is time for the Saints to work. The Lord did not entrust this great work to anyone but entrusted it to the disciples who experienced the faith of the cross and resurrection. Today, the mission of the gospel witness is to those of us who have the faith of the cross and the resurrection. The Lord searches for people who are in need in those days and gives them the gospel of God. That is why we continue to keep the ministry of the gospel unbroken. No matter how unbelievers attack the church and interfere with God's ministry, the propagation of the gospel will exist to the end of world. There is a saying in the Bible that it moves the candlestick.

Our God is the one who moves the candlestick of our mission. In the past, missionaries in foreign countries were mostly in charge of evangelism and mission work. Many supported them as missionaries. However, with the rise of atheists such as humanism, the development of science and civilization, the church is attacked and many abandon their faith.

We must realize that if we are not awake and cannot keep up with the mission of the church, the candlesticks and lamps of our ministry can move into the revival of the church around us.

We must be a church that prepares for the second coming of the Lord so that this holy and blessed mission will not be in vain. That is why the Lord must come. The Lord is looking for again. He is looking for his Saints again. The Lord will surely come again to destroy the devil's power and give the Saints an eternal victory.

What is the sign that will appear at the end?

First, it is an increase in knowledge as a sign of the end (Daniel 12:4). In the 1900s, research has shown that the rate of knowledge increase over the period of about 110 years has increased by more than 10 times from the pre-1900s to the creation period. What does this mean? As we enter the modern world, our knowledge increases rapidly.

After a day, new knowledge, doctrines, and research pour out. The earth is narrowing to one living zone. We can go to the other side of the world for a day. What does this mean? It means to be a global village. The word 'globalization' has two good meanings and a bad one. In a good sense, it means that the preaching of the gospel will go as fast as that.

In the past, if you were going to the mission, you had to sail for a few months on a boat.

But now, the Internet, airplanes, etc. are developed and information goes to wherever you want.

In bad terms, evil iniquities spread quickly. It easily corrupts people. A bad thing means it spreads that fast. Second, the Antichrist will emerge (Matthew 24:5). Many people deceive all the world by saying that antichrist is the Holy Spirit of the Comforter, who is Jesus. Third, wars, famines, sickness, and earthquakes arise (Matthew 24:7).

Earthquakes in many parts of the globe cause tens of thousands to die and hundreds of thousands to die of famine. Fourth, there will be persecution (Matthew 24:9). "Ye shall be hated by all nations for my name" Fifth, false prophets are active (Matthew 24:11). False prophets do illegal acts. They teach the word wrongly, false truth, guiding sheep in the wrong way. Sixth, illegal acts are prevalent (Matthew 24:12). Seventh, love is cooled (Matthew 24:12). Eighth, the gospel spreads rapidly (Matthew 24:14). As the world gets worse and harder, the speed with which to accept the word gets faster. Ninth, the Gospel spreads rapidly. The devil will become even more proud. Just to get in the way. Evidence of 'apostasy' arises from that evidence. The tenth, the saints are fallen (2 Tim. 3: 1-5); self-love, love of money, pride, blasphemy, rebellion, not grateful.

What are the attitudes of the Saints to the Second Coming covenant and to the end? (Job 19:25, 26)

Let's think about these words.

Let us not be deceived (Matthew 24:5).
We must filter out the sounds of sin and heresy that deceive us.
Let's preach the Gospel (Matthew 24:14).
"The gospel of the kingdom shall be preached throughout the world to be a witness unto all nations."
Let us forget the folly of the world (Matthew 24:18).
"He who is in the field, do not turn back to pick up the robe."
Let's wait in reserve (Matthew 24:44).

"Be ready, for the Son of Man will come when you do not think."

Let's be awake! (Matthew 25:13).

"Therefore, keep watch. You do not know that day and its time."

Let us live a loyal life (Matthew 25: 28-30).

Let us not lose a talent but fulfill our mission with loyalty.

Let us endure trouble (Luke 21:19).

"Your patience will gain your soul."

Let us live by always thinking of the Lord (Romans 3: 11, 12).

There is no one to understand, no one to seek God.

Let us be clean (Romans 13:12-14).

There is none who does good, neither is there any.

Do not be afraid (2 Thess. 2:1-3).

When the day of the Lord has come, you must not easily shake or fear or do not.

Let us work together (Hebrews 10:25).

Encourage love and good deeds

Let us restraint and pray (1 Peter 4:7).

The end of all things is at hand;

Let us repent and wait (2 Peter 3:9, 15).

Longsuffering against you, that none may perish,

Let's pray for the Lord's return (Revelation 22:20).

"The one who testified about these things said, I will come quickly. Amen, Lord Jesus."

The conclusion of the covenant is that God restores everything. This world God created will be restored by the salvation of Jesus Christ and will lead the saints in hope.

The Covenants of God

{Genesis 2: 16-17, 3:15}

16 And the Lord God commanded the man, saying, "You may surely eat of every tree of the garden, 17 but of the tree of the knowledge of good and evil you shall not eat, for in the day that you eat of it you shall surely die."

Genesis 3:15 "I will put enmity between you and the woman, and between your offspring and her offspring he shall bruise your head, and you shall bruise his heel."

In the beginning, God created the heavens and the earth and made mankind. And he made them a garden and dwelt therein. The man was to be protected by God and to live according to God's purpose. God made a covenant with man and wanted to be their God.

The fall/ Genesis 3:22-24

22 Then the Lord God said, "Behold, the man has become like one of us in knowing good and evil. Now, lest he reach out his hand and take also of the tree of life and eat, and live forever" 23 therefore the Lord God sent him out from the garden of Eden to work the ground from which he was taken. 24 He drove out the man, and at the east of the Garden of Eden he placed the cherubim and a flaming sword that turned every way to guard the way to the tree of life.

{Genesis 9: 8-17}

8 Then God said to Noah and to his sons with him: 9 "I now establish my covenant with you and with your descendants after you 10 and with every living creature that was with you—the birds, the livestock and all the wild animals, all those that came out of the ark with you—every living creature on earth. 11 I establish my covenant with you: Never again will all life be destroyed by the waters of a flood; never again will there be a flood to destroy the earth."

12 And God said, "This is the sign of the covenant I am making between me and you and every living creature with you, a covenant for all generations to come: 13 I have set my rainbow in the clouds, and it will be the sign of the covenant between me and the earth. 14 Whenever I bring clouds over the earth and the rainbow appears in the clouds, 15 I will remember my covenant between me and you and all living creatures of every kind. Never again will the waters become a flood to destroy all life. 16 Whenever the rainbow appears in the clouds, I will see it and remember the everlasting covenant between God and all living creatures of every kind on the earth."

17 So God said to Noah, "This is the sign of the covenant I have established between me and all life on the earth."

God heals the wound forgets and forgives our sins. Through promise, God gives us unlimited opportunities and hope.

The Covenants of God

{Genesis 15:12-21}

12 as the sun was setting, Abram fell into a deep sleep, and a thick and dreadful darkness came over him. 13 Then the Lord said to him, "Know for certain that for four hundred years your descendants will be strangers in a country not their own and that they will be enslaved and mistreated there. 14 But I will punish the nation they serve as slaves, and afterward they will come out with great possessions. 15 You, however, will go to your ancestors in peace and be buried at a good old age. 16 In the fourth generation, your descendants will come back here, for the sin of the Amorites has not yet reached its full measure."

17 When the sun had set and darkness had fallen, a smoking firepot with a blazing torch appeared and passed between the pieces. 18 On that day the Lord made a covenant with Abram and said, "To your descendants I give this land, from the Wadi[a] of Egypt to the great river, the Euphrates— 19 the land of the Kenites, Kenizzites, Kadmonites, 20 Hittites, Perizzites, Rephaites, 21 Amorites, Canaanites, Girgashites, and Jebusites."

God is the center of our lives. He is with us in all our lives and has dominated us. When we live in the center of God, we have a purpose of being.

{Genesis 17: 1-21}

13 Whether born in your household or bought with your money, they must be circumcised. My covenant in your flesh is to be an everlasting covenant. 14 Any uncircumcised male, who has not been circumcised in the flesh, will be cut off from his people; he has broken my covenant."

15 God also said to Abraham, "As for Sarai your wife, you are no longer to call her Sarai; her name will be Sarah. 16 I will bless her and will surely give you a son by her. I will bless her so that she will be the mother of nations; kings of peoples will come from her."

17 Abraham fell facedown; he laughed and said to himself, "Will a son be born to a man a hundred years old? Will Sarah bear a child at the age of ninety?" 18 And Abraham said to God, "If only Ishmael might live under your blessing!"

19 Then God said, "Yes, but your wife Sarah will bear you a son, and you will call him Isaac. I will establish my covenant with him as an everlasting covenant for his descendants after him. 20 And as for Ishmael, I have heard you: I will surely bless him; I will make him fruitful and will greatly increase his numbers. He will be the father of twelve rulers, and I will make him into a great nation. 21 But my covenant I will establish with Isaac, whom Sarah will bear to you by this time next year."

We are God's possessed people. We must separate and live according to the will of God.

The Covenants of God

13 There above it stood the Lord, and he said: "I am the Lord, the God of your father Abraham and the God of Isaac. I will give you and your descendants the land on which you are lying. 14 Your descendants will be like the dust of the earth, and you will spread out to the west and to the east, to the north and to the south. All peoples on earth will be blessed through you and your offspring. 15 I am with you and will watch over you wherever you go, and I will bring you back to this land. I will not leave you until I have done what I have promised you."

16 When Jacob awoke from his sleep, he thought, "Surely the Lord is in this place, and I was not aware of it." 17 He was afraid and said, "How awesome is this place! This is none other than the house of God; this is the gate of heaven."

18 Early the next morning Jacob took the stone he had placed under his head and set it up as a pillar and poured oil on top of it. 19 He called that place Bethel, though the city used to be called Luz.

20 Then Jacob made a vow, saying, "If God will be with me and will watch over me on this journey I am taking and will give me food to eat and clothes to wear 21 so that I return safely to my father's household, then the Lord will be my God 22 and[e] this stone that I have set up as a pillar will be God's house, and of all that you give me I will give you a tenth."

God protects the Saints. He keeps us through sure promises and guides our way

{Exdodus 20:1-17}
The Ten Commandments

[2] I am the LORD your God, who brought you out of the land of Egypt, out of the house of slavery. [3] You shall not have other gods beside me. [4] You shall not make for yourself an idol or a likeness of anything in the heavens above or on the earth below or in the waters beneath the earth; [5] you shall not bow down before them or serve them. For I, the LORD, your God, am a jealous God, inflicting punishment for their ancestors' wickedness on the children of those who hate me, down to the third and fourth generation; [6] but showing love down to the thousandth generation of those who love me and keep my commandments. [7] You shall not invoke the name of the LORD, your God, in vain. For the LORD will not leave unpunished anyone who invokes his name in vain. [8] Remember the sabbath day—keep it holy. [9] Six days you may labor and do all your work, [10] but the seventh day is a sabbath of the LORDyour God. You shall not do any work, either you, your son or your daughter, your male or female slave, your work animal, or the resident alien within your gates. [11] For in six days the LORD made the heavens and the earth, the sea and all that is in them; but on the seventh day he rested. That is why the LORD has blessed the sabbath day and made it holy. [12] Honor your father and your mother, that you may have a long life in the land the LORD your God is giving you. [13] You shall not kill. [14] You shall not commit adultery. [15] You shall not steal. [16] You shall not bear false witness against your neighbor. [17] You shall not covet your neighbor's house. You shall not covet your neighbor's wife, his male or female slave, his ox or donkey, or anything that belongs to your neighbor.

The Covenants of God

{Numbers 18:19-20}

19 As a perpetual due I assign to you and to your sons and daughters with you all the contributions of holy things which the Israelites set aside for the Lord; this is a covenant of salt to last forever before the Lord, for you and for your descendants with you. 20 Then the Lord said to Aaron: You shall not have any heritage in their land nor hold any portion among them; I will be your portion and your heritage among the Israelites.

The Lord wants us to live apart from the world. He wants to live according to God's character holiness. However, the Saints must serve as Christians in the world. It is not irresponsibility toward the world, but standing on the Word and proclaiming the justice of God.

{Numbers 25:10-13}

10 Then the Lord said to Moses: 11 Phinehas, son of Eleazar, son of Aaron the priest, has turned my anger from the Israelites by his being as jealous among them as I am; that is why I did not put an end to the Israelites in my jealousy. 12 Announce, therefore, that I hereby give him my covenant of peace, 13 which shall be for him and for his descendants after him the covenant of an everlasting priesthood, because he was jealous on behalf of his God and thus made expiation for the Israelites.

Through Jesus Christ's righteous deeds, all our sins have been removed. We are royal priests. We are those who have received new positions such as Phinehas.

The Covenants of God

{Deuteronomy 29:1-30:10}

These are the terms of the covenant the Lord commanded Moses to make with the Israelites in Moab, in addition to the covenant he had made with them at Horeb. 2 Moses summoned all the Israelites and said to them: Your eyes have seen all that the Lord did in Egypt to Pharaoh, to all his officials and to all his land. 3 With your own eyes you saw those great trials, those signs and great wonders. 4 But to this day the Lord has not given you a mind that understands or eyes that see or ears that hear. 5 Yet the Lord says, "During the forty years that I led you through the wilderness, your clothes did not wear out, nor did the sandals on your feet. 6 You ate no bread and drank no wine or other fermented drink. I did this so that you might know that I am the Lord your God." 7 When you reached this place, Sihon king of Heshbon and Og king of Bashan came out to fight against us, but we defeated them. 8 We took their land and gave it as an inheritance to the Reubenites, the Gadites and the half-tribe of Manasseh. 9 Carefully follow the terms of this covenant, so that you may prosper in everything you do. 10 All of you are standing today in the presence of the Lord your God—your leaders and chief men, your elders and officials, and all the other men of Israel, 11 together with your children and your wives, and the foreigners living in your camps who chop your wood and carry your water. 12 You are standing here in order to enter into a covenant with the Lord your God, a covenant the Lord is making with you this day and sealing with an oath, 13 to confirm you this day as his people, that he may be your God as he promised you and as he swore to your fathers, Abraham, Isaac and Jacob. 14 I am making this covenant, with its oath, not only with you 15 who are standing here with us today in the presence of the Lord our God but also with those who are not here today.

The Covenants of God

{2 Samuel 7:8-17}

8 "Now then, tell my servant David, 'This is what the Lord Almighty says: I took you from the pasture, from tending the flock, and appointed you ruler over my people Israel. 9 I have been with you wherever you have gone, and I have cut off all your enemies from before you. Now I will make your name great, like the names of the greatest men on earth. 10 And I will provide a place for my people Israel and will plant them so that they can have a home of their own and no longer be disturbed. Wicked people will not oppress them anymore, as they did at the beginning 11 and have done ever since the time I appointed leaders over my people Israel. I will also give you rest from all your enemies.

David is only a stepping stone of redemption. On the most important road to Jesus Christ is King David. We only need to know David to know Jesus Christ.

{Jeremiah 31:31-34}

31 Behold, the days come, saith the Lord, that I will make a new covenant with the house of Israel, and with the house of Judah: 32 Not according to the covenant that I made with their fathers in the day that I took them by the hand to bring them out of the land of Egypt; which my covenant they brake, although I was an husband unto them, saith the Lord: 33 But this shall be the covenant that I will make with the house of Israel; After those days, saith the Lord, I will put my law in their inward parts, and write it in their hearts; and will be their God, and they shall be my people. 34 And they shall teach no more every man his neighbour, and every man his brother, saying, Know the Lord: for they shall all know me, from the least of them unto the greatest of them, saith the Lord: for I will forgive their iniquity, and I will remember their sin no more.

The Covenants of God

26 And as they were eating, Jesus took bread, and blessed it, and brake it, and gave it to the disciples, and said, Take, eat; this is my body.

27 And he took the cup, and gave thanks, and gave it to them, saying, Drink ye all of it;

28 For this is my blood of the new testament, which is shed for many for the remission of sins.

29 But I say unto you, I will not drink henceforth of this fruit of the vine, until that day when I drink it new with you in my Father's kingdom.

{John 16:7-15}

7 Nevertheless I tell you the truth. It is to your advantage that I go away; for if I do not go away, the Helper will not come to you; but if I depart, I will send Him to you. 8 And when He has come, He will convict the world of sin, and of righteousness, and of judgment: 9 of sin, because they do not believe in Me; 10 of righteousness, because I go to My Father and you see Me no more; 11 of judgment, because the ruler of this world is judged.

12 "I still have many things to say to you, but you cannot bear them now. 13 However, when He, the Spirit of truth, has come, He will guide you into all truth; for He will not speak on His own authority, but whatever He hears He will speak; and He will tell you things to come. 14 He will glorify Me, for He will take of what is Mine and declare it to you. 15 All things that the Father has are Mine. Therefore I said that He will take of Mine and declare it to you.

The Covenants of God

{Luke 21:20-28}

20 But when you see Jerusalem surrounded by armies, then know that its desolation has come near. 21 Then let those who are in Judea flee to the mountains, and let those who are inside the city depart, and let not those who are out in the country enter it; 22 for these are days of vengeance, to fulfill all that is written. 23 Alas for those who are with child and for those who give suck in those days! For great distress shall be upon the earth and wrath upon this people; 24 they will fall by the edge of the sword, and be led captive among all nations; and Jerusalem will be trodden down by the Gentiles, until the times of the Gentiles are fulfilled.

25 And there will be signs in sun and moon and stars, and upon the earth distress of nations in perplexity at the roaring of the sea and the waves, 26 men fainting with fear and with foreboding of what is coming on the world; for the powers of the heavens will be shaken. 27 And then they will see the Son of man coming in a cloud with power and great glory. 28 Now when these things begin to take place, look up and raise your heads, because your redemption is drawing near.

YONGJEA JOHN HAN

ACKNOWLEDGEMENT

THIS BOOK IS WRITTEN FOR THE WEAK AND THEIR MISSION OF NORTH AMERICA. JESUS ALWAYS STOOD ON THE SIDE OF THE WEAK PEOPLE OF THE EARTH AND PREACHED THE JUSTICE OF GOD AND HIS KINGDOM. ESPECIALLY I WOULD LIKE TO EXPRESS MY SINCERE THANKS TO ALL THE DIRECTORS, PASTOR PARK JONG IK, CHOI SUN HWA, CHO JIN HEUI OF THE LIVING BREATH (SOOM) MISSION SOCIETY THAT PRAYED FOR THE MINISTRIES.

102

Yongjea John Han majored in Law and English Literature, majoring in theology in the Netherlands and the United States and Honam Presbyterian Theological Seminary. He also worked as a poet and writer in Korea. He then moved to Canada to continue his work as a writer and missionary. He and his wife and two children, near BC, are dedicated to a mission for the weak and writing activities.

[Books: *Slow City, The Space, Refugees, The Old Memories of Tynehead, The Qs about the Alists, Refugees Ali, Hastings Street, Epistles from the Drifters1, The Living Breath, The Covenants of God, Theology for the weak, The Justice of the World Churches, Are You Breathing with God? Jesus On the side of the Weak*]